A journal for turning Thirty

Created for you by Tatum Winslow

A note from me to you

Well, hello there! Looks like someone is about to turn 30! This can be "no big deal" for some, but for others, it can be a major milestone whether for good or ill.

As I was staring down my 30th birthday, I decided I wanted to ease myself in by commemorating it all year long. I created a list of 30 goals I wanted to accomplish before my 30th birthday. They ranged from lofty to simple; however, each were important to me. As I accomplished each goal, I felt proud and excited! I documented my journey so that I could remember my achievements and the feelings they gave me. The actual event of turning 30 became more than just a birthday. It was a celebration of all that I learned and gained in my 30th year. It made me excited for a new decade of life.

I wanted to share my process with others who are approaching this time of their life. Turning 30 can raise various emotions in people. Whatever your feelings, my hope is that this journal will help you also feel prepared and even joyous in this milestone. You have got this. You are ready!

Sincerely, Tatum

How to use this planner

Section 1:

List out your goals for your 30th year. Be sure to create a few backup ideas as well! You never know where life is going to take you.

Section 2:

Write down your reflections on the past decade. Record your thoughts on the advent of a new one.

Section 3:

Make plans to accomplish your 30 before 30 goals! Decide on the 'what', 'when', 'where', and 'how'.

Section 4:

This is a calendar section to help you keep track of important plans and dates. There are also pages for monthly intentions and self evaluation!

Section 5:

As you complete your goals, write about the experience! Share the details and your thoughts on each adventure.

Section 6:

Jot down your final impressions. What did you learn from your 30 before 30? What does the future have in store for you?

Welcome to your 30th year!

30

before

30

goals

- Your adventures start here -

1

2

3

4

5

6

- Embrace it, my dear -

7

8

9

10

11

12

- Living can happen today -

13

14

15

16

17

18

- It's never too late -

19

20

21

22

23

24

- So go and live great -

25

26

27

28

29

30

For your

30th

year's underway

Time for Plan B

'List a few more possible adventures'

Reflections

What did you achieve in your 20s?

What are you most excited about
for your 30s?

What do you hope to accomplish

before turning 40?

Make a plan

Use this section to plan out your

30 before 30 goals

What

When

Where

How

2

What

When

Where

How

What

When

Where

How

_____

What

_____

When

_____

Where

_____

How

5

What

When

Where

How

What

_____

When

_____

Where

_____

How

1

What

When

Where

How

What

When

Where

How

What

When

Where

How

10

What

When

Where

How

11

What

When

Where

How

12

What

When

Where

How

13

What

When

Where

How

14

What

When

Where

How

15

What

When

Where

How

What

_____

When

_____

Where

_____

How

_____

11

What

When

Where

How

What

_____

When

_____

Where

_____

How

11

What

When

Where

How

20

What

When

Where

How

21

What

When

Where

How

22

What

When

Where

How

23

_____

What

_____

When

_____

Where

_____

How

24

What

When

Where

How

25

What

When

Where

How

26

What

When

Where

How

27

What

When

Where

How

21

What

When

Where

How

21

What

When

Where

How

30

What

When

Where

How

Calendar

Monthly Plans

- ◯ _____
- ◯ _____
- ◯ _____
- ◯ _____
- ◯ _____
- ◯ _____
- ◯ _____
- ◯ _____
- ◯ _____

Month/Year

Sun	Mon	Tue	Wed	Thu	Fri	Sat

Monthly Evaluation

What goals did you meet?

What are you proud of this month?

Monthly Evaluation

What will you do differently next month?

Monthly Plans

- ◯ _____
- ◯ _____
- ◯ _____
- ◯ _____
- ◯ _____
- ◯ _____
- ◯ _____
- ◯ _____
- ◯ _____

Month/Year

Sun	Mon	Tue	Wed	Thu	Fri	Sat

Monthly Evaluation

What goals did you meet?

What are you proud of this month?

Monthly Evaluation

What will you do differently next month?

Monthly Plans

- ◯ _____
- ◯ _____
- ◯ _____
- ◯ _____
- ◯ _____
- ◯ _____
- ◯ _____
- ◯ _____
- ◯ _____

Month/Year

Sun	Mon	Tue	Wed	Thu	Fri	Sat

Monthly Evaluation

What goals did you meet?

What are you proud of this month?

Monthly Evaluation

What will you do differently next month?

Monthly Plans

- ○ _____
- ○ _____
- ○ _____
- ○ _____
- ○ _____
- ○ _____
- ○ _____
- ○ _____
- ○ _____

Month/Year

Sun	Mon	Tue	Wed	Thu	Fri	Sat

Monthly Evaluation

What goals did you meet?

What are you proud of this month?

Monthly Evaluation

What will you do differently next month?

Monthly Plans

- ○ _____
- ○ _____
- ○ _____
- ○ _____
- ○ _____
- ○ _____
- ○ _____
- ○ _____
- ○ _____

Month/Year

Sun	Mon	Tue	Wed	Thu	Fri	Sat

Monthly Evaluation

What goals did you meet?

What are you proud of this month?

Monthly Evaluation

What will you do differently next month?

Monthly Plans

- ○ _____
- ○ _____
- ○ _____
- ○ _____
- ○ _____
- ○ _____
- ○ _____
- ○ _____
- ○ _____

Month/Year

Sun	Mon	Tue	Wed	Thu	Fri	Sat

Monthly Evaluation

What goals did you meet?

What are you proud of this month?

Monthly Evaluation

What will you do differently next month?

Monthly Plans

- ◯ _____
- ◯ _____
- ◯ _____
- ◯ _____
- ◯ _____
- ◯ _____
- ◯ _____
- ◯ _____
- ◯ _____

Month/Year

Sun	Mon	Tue	Wed	Thu	Fri	Sat

Monthly Evaluation

What goals did you meet?

What are you proud of this month?

Monthly Evaluation

What will you do differently next month?

Monthly Plans

- ○ _____
- ○ _____
- ○ _____
- ○ _____
- ○ _____
- ○ _____
- ○ _____
- ○ _____
- ○ _____

Month/Year

Sun	Mon	Tue	Wed	Thu	Fri	Sat

Monthly Evaluation

What goals did you meet?

What are you proud of this month?

Monthly Evaluation

What will you do differently next month?

Monthly Plans

- ○ _____
- ○ _____
- ○ _____
- ○ _____
- ○ _____
- ○ _____
- ○ _____
- ○ _____
- ○ _____

Month/Year

Sun	Mon	Tue	Wed	Thu	Fri	Sat

Monthly Plans

- ⭕ _____
- ⭕ _____
- ⭕ _____
- ⭕ _____
- ⭕ _____
- ⭕ _____
- ⭕ _____
- ⭕ _____
- ⭕ _____

Month/Year

Sun	Mon	Tue	Wed	Thu	Fri	Sat

Monthly Evaluation

What goals did you meet?

What are you proud of this month?

Monthly Evaluation

What will you do differently next month?

Monthly Plans

- ○ _____
- ○ _____
- ○ _____
- ○ _____
- ○ _____
- ○ _____
- ○ _____
- ○ _____
- ○ _____

Month/Year

Sun	Mon	Tue	Wed	Thu	Fri	Sat

Monthly Evaluation

What goals did you meet?

What are you proud of this month?

Monthly Evaluation

What will you do differently next month?

Monthly Plans

- ○ _____
- ○ _____
- ○ _____
- ○ _____
- ○ _____
- ○ _____
- ○ _____
- ○ _____
- ○ _____

Month/Year

Sun	Mon	Tue	Wed	Thu	Fri	Sat

Monthly Evaluation

What goals did you meet?

What are you proud of this month?

Monthly Evaluation

What will you do differently next month?

Monthly Plans

- ◯ _____
- ◯ _____
- ◯ _____
- ◯ _____
- ◯ _____
- ◯ _____
- ◯ _____
- ◯ _____
- ◯ _____

Month/Year

Sun	Mon	Tue	Wed	Thu	Fri	Sat

Monthly Evaluation

What goals did you meet?

What are you proud of this month?

Monthly Evaluation

What will you do differently next month?

Mission Complete!

Use this section to write about the goals you accomplished

1

Which adventure is this?

When did you accomplish it?

Who was with you?

Where did you go?

How was it?

2

Which adventure is this?

When did you accomplish it?

Who was with you?

Where did you go?

How was it?

3

Which adventure is this?

When did you accomplish it?

Who was with you?

Where did you go?

How was it?

4

Which adventure is this?

When did you accomplish it?

Who was with you?

Where did you go?

How was it?

5

Which adventure is this?

When did you accomplish it?

Who was with you?

Where did you go?

How was it?

Which adventure is this?

When did you accomplish it?

Who was with you?

Where did you go?

How was it?

7

Which adventure is this?

When did you accomplish it?

Who was with you?

Where did you go?

How was it?

Which adventure is this?

When did you accomplish it?

Who was with you?

Where did you go?

How was it?

1

Which adventure is this?

When did you accomplish it?

Who was with you?

Where did you go?

How was it?

10

Which adventure is this?

When did you accomplish it?

Who was with you?

Where did you go?

How was it?

11

Which adventure is this?

When did you accomplish it?

Who was with you?

Where did you go?

How was it?

12

Which adventure is this?

When did you accomplish it?

Who was with you?

Where did you go?

How was it?

13

Which adventure is this?

When did you accomplish it?

Who was with you?

Where did you go?

How was it?

14

Which adventure is this?

When did you accomplish it?

Who was with you?

Where did you go?

How was it?

15

Which adventure is this?

When did you accomplish it?

Who was with you?

Where did you go?

How was it?

16

Which adventure is this?

When did you accomplish it?

Who was with you?

Where did you go?

How was it?

17

Which adventure is this?

When did you accomplish it?

Who was with you?

Where did you go?

How was it?

11

Which adventure is this?

When did you accomplish it?

Who was with you?

Where did you go?

How was it?

11

Which adventure is this?

When did you accomplish it?

Who was with you?

Where did you go?

How was it?

20

Which adventure is this?

When did you accomplish it?

Who was with you?

Where did you go?

How was it?

21

Which adventure is this?

When did you accomplish it?

Who was with you?

Where did you go?

How was it?

22

Which adventure is this?

When did you accomplish it?

Who was with you?

Where did you go?

How was it?

23

Which adventure is this?

When did you accomplish it?

Who was with you?

Where did you go?

How was it?

24

Which adventure is this?

When did you accomplish it?

Who was with you?

Where did you go?

How was it?

25

Which adventure is this?

When did you accomplish it?

Who was with you?

Where did you go?

How was it?

26

Which adventure is this?

When did you accomplish it?

Who was with you?

Where did you go?

How was it?

27

Which adventure is this?

When did you accomplish it?

Who was with you?

Where did you go?

How was it?

21

Which adventure is this?

When did you accomplish it?

Who was with you?

Where did you go?

How was it?

21

Which adventure is this?

When did you accomplish it?

Who was with you?

Where did you go?

How was it?

30

Which adventure is this?

When did you accomplish it?

Who was with you?

Where did you go?

How was it?

Final

Thoughts

What did you think of your 30th year?

What did you learn?

How did you grow?

What are you looking forward to
next year?

Dear 30s,

I'm ready for you.

Made in the USA
Coppell, TX
26 October 2023

23387385R00085